YOUR ART IS BULLSH*T

a handbook for revolutionary art

BY MICHAEL REYNOLDS

LET ME REITTERATE

YOUR ART IS BULLSH*T

BY MICHAEL REYNOLDS

Preface

If you're looking for the next best youtube clip of "tips and tricks to running a six-figure art business" then kindly close this book, start a small fire in the middle of your living room, and toss this book into that fire because that's the only way this book is going to leave you feeling warm at the end.

I'm not here to be your pot o' gold at the end of the unicorn's rainbow. I'm not here to tell you a happy story that will leave you feeling good and in turn somehow make you a more profitable student of capitalism. I'm also not here to write you a virtual hug and congratulation that leaves you feeling the warm fuzzies of your self-indulgent narcissism.

If anything, I'm here to tell you the story of cynicism, the death of the idea of community, and the watering down of art.

    Though please, as always, subscribe for more content like this, and don't forget to SMASH that like button. It does help me so greatly and if you made it this far, thank you so much for being a supporter. I love you all, and until the next episode. Goodbye.

Chapter One

"Always punch up, never punch down."

I've been a photographer for the last fifteen years. About three years ago I picked up other art mediums including acrylic painting, digital painting, compositing, and some random craft-making. There hasn't been a day in those fifteen years where I haven't made some attempt to create, or be creative, or immerse myself in the creations of others.

I've made hundreds of thousands of photographs and hundreds of art pieces between my digital work and paintings. Hell, I even took up making perfumes, beard oils, and candles to keep my need to create sated. After that much time in the field, and then the now years spent doing photography and art as a career I find myself needing to quote the words of John Coffey from the underappreciated film "The Green Mile"

"I'm tired, boss. Tired of being on the road, lonely as a sparrow in the rain. I'm tired of never having me a buddy to be with, to tell me where we's going to, coming from, or why. Mostly, I'm tired of people being ugly to each other. I'm tired of all the pain I feel and hear in the world, every day. There's too much of it. It's like pieces of glass in my head, all the time."

"Pieces of glass in my head, all the time." is an apt summarization of the way I feel when I look out onto the vast sea of, what feels to be, intentionally mediocre, banal, repetitious, and conformist capital-driven artists that I see from day to day. This of course doesn't even touch on the grasping, backbiting, petty, selfish, and downright abusive antics that frequent the art community.

If social media and the internet have taught me anything about people, it's that it would be an easier and more productive life to dwell in a discarded tin can in a muddy ditch somewhere than to live under the constant barrage of negativity that infests the online space.

I was diagnosed with bipolar type 2 at the beginning of 2021. I know, big shocker from the guy who just spent the first five hundred words of his book berating and screaming into the void, but being diagnosed helped me single out, and be acutely aware of how harmful the internet, and communities I frequented on it, were being.

See, in the online artist's lexicon, we've created entire sentences to defend a lack of effort such as "we all start somewhere", or "as long as you like it, it's art". I personally despise that last one. I get it, be happy with the things you make, and that is such a huge part of why you should make art, but art has a proper definition that I like to stand by that says art is something created with intention and skill.

However, at the same time we've weaponized statements such as "I'm not being mean, I'm just being blunt" and "I'm just being honest" As if we couldn't be honest without also being so harsh that we crush people's dreams and hopes like glass crunching and trodden under our heals.

Honestly, I feel like the young and aspiring artists are always the most judged, trampled, and suffocated creators in the sphere. They come in, they know nothing but excitement at this fresh and fun new hobby, only to be dogpiled by other new artists, old artists, elitists, and gatekeepers alike.

At the end of the day, we should EXPECT new creatives to produce less than aesthetic photographs, paintings, crafts, etc. They haven't stretched their creative muscles yet. They haven't refined their pen strokes. More fortunately, they haven't been calloused over by the "instructions" and berating of the "long-timers".

On the opposite spectrum, you have the artists that have been doing this for years. The elites. The ones that have invested the time and sweat into refining their work. Don't worry, if you don't know which ones they are, they'll be sure to tell you and fast. They'll wave around their awards received from decades past and drone on about how art was done back then, and how it should be done now.

What about the quality of their work though? It's shiny, sure. The strokes are refined, the images follow the rules. Their creations conform to what we have all been conditioned to accept as "good". Yet I can't help but feel that the best artists are the most derivative and watered down of them all because they've spent ten or more years stuck in the same rut making the same art over and over and over again. Like telling a joke and getting some laughs so you keep telling the same joke for the next twenty years, except it's not funny anymore. Please, for the love of everything, make something new. Tell a new joke already.

See, my mental health diagnosis made me acutely more aware of what I consume, how I consume, and why I consume on the internet and in my day-to-day interactions. The resulting conclusion that I came to is that I can be the harshest critic, the snidest, sharpest, condescending, and most damaging voice of them all. Somewhere along the line of climbing my way over others in an attempt to be "the best", or really, "the loudest" artist I could be, I had forgotten the basics of "Always punch up, never punch down."

I've destroyed and crushed the spirits of hundreds of artists without even the smallest bit of exaggeration. I argue, well, and at length. I'm good at picking apart people's defenses and rebuttals and striking where I know it hurts. I've weaponized critique to a point where I can even get away with doing it and all to the thunderous applause of the crowd. Meanwhile, someone on the receiving end is coming into contact with possibly their first interaction with public shaming, and from what was supposed to bring them joy.

It's easy to bully a child. That's why we feel the urge to protect them as they grow up. They're defenseless, feeble, and unassuming. They often see the best in the world with a wide-eyed naivete. That translates into them being easy victims. When those children become adults though, and they pick up that paintbrush for the first time in fresh amazement, we forget that they're in the infantile stages of creation, and we set out to quickly break their spirits before they can get too far off course from where we believe they should be.

I don't think art is beyond criticism. I don't just think anything goes. I don't think you should blow smoke up someone's ass just to keep them in good spirits but I've chosen that for the rest of this book, and in my personal life, to choose a different target. See, if you punch down you're only digging a deeper hole. It's like attacking a defenseless child. When you punch up you can raise the standard of what's considered "the top." You punch up to remove the stagnant artists and push them to either make progress or get out of the way.

If you're new to the industry or are just picking up your hobbyist skill in the field of art, come along and let's see where this goes. I'll try not to hammer on you too much. However, If you've been doing this a while and you're feeling pretty successful right about now, I'll reiterate my opening statement and tell you to burn this book. It'll be better for you to have that charred reminder on your living room floor than to endure the rest of this book thinking that I'm going to be on your side or say anything in here that won't leave you feeling burned just as well.

Chapter Two
"They will chop you down just to count your rings"

So you've been doing this a while. You've got the skills, the time invested, the personal experience from living the craft vs just philosophizing about it. Well, that's all well and good. Slow clap for you and all the grand things you've accomplished. Here's just an idea though.

Your art is bullshit.

It's bad. I'm serious. It's harder to follow along with than the extended three-hour cut of Avatar (The blue people one, not The Last Airbender movie adaptation. Though, that was a tough watch too but for different reasons.)

See, you're so full of yourself. So full of doing what works that you stopped trying the things that might not. Your art smells like a pond that hasn't had moving water for the last decade. Creativity isn't repetition. It's not learning how to do one thing and then beating that same dead horse into oblivion.

By definition, you're not a creative person anymore. You're like a redundant robot. About as interesting as, I don't know, the next million artists doing various iterations of the exact thing you're doing. Maybe you forgot that though. There are millions of artists doing exactly what you're doing and yet somehow in a world population of billions, you feel special like you somehow reached the summit.

Like, come on, a portrait of a person standing in a field with a blown-out sky and the background blurred into total abstraction? Boring as hell. Lame. That probably offends you, but your lack of motivation to progress is offending me so we're even or something. You're using the standards as a crutch.

Photographers use bokeh as a crutch for their piss poor composition and storytelling abilities. Do you know what's more satisfying than bokeh? A background. Do you know what's more difficult than isolating your subject with bokeh? Composing a busy image where all the background elements contribute to the story you're trying to tell about your subject.

Instead, Modern images are just endings to stories we never read.

Imagine opening up a book that you've been waiting to read and as you get to it you realize you already know the ending. Imagine that the first sentence tells you the ending, and then for 600 pages it just repeats that ending over and over again. Though I'm sure someone would try to market this as art, that would be a pretty lame story, right? Beyond just being a bad story you would probably feel a little angry as well. It would feel as if you were just stolen from. You set out to find adventure only to have it crushed before it ever started.

As horrible as that may sound for literature we do this all the time in Photography and the greater field of art. We set out to take a photo, make a painting, make a sculpture, and we pay no mind to how to tell a story or compose a thought-provoking image. We center up our subject in the frame and there's your ending.

We've become the energy drink ads of the art community. Flashy, loud, and just screaming the obvious subject at you. Good creations, like good stories, need the tension of the unknown to lead us through the winding and mysterious narrative to our final subject, to the point. Apart from this, our creations become uninteresting for anything more than a glance as we swipe past them along with tons of other endings on our Instagram feed or other social media.

We've simplified art down to something easy to consume. Like some chips, we treat Instagram like a can of pringles. "Once you pop, the fun don't stop" or more appropriately, once you swipe there's nothing with any kind of originality worth stopping for. Art was supposed to make us feel something, have something to discuss, confront some idea or emotion wasn't it?

Instead, we refine art into the white bread of skills. Uniform, bland, and bleached of any nutritional value. This makes it so anything that stands out becomes an easy target. "Tall poppy syndrome" makes us critical of anything exceptional, or exceptionally bad. Quick to attack anything that doesn't conform.

What are you going to leave behind though? A quote from Aesop Rock pops into my head from time to time. "They will chop you down just to count your rings". When they chop you down what will they find?

Dendrochronology: "the science or technique of dating events, environmental change, and archaeological artifacts by using the characteristic patterns of annual growth rings in timber and tree trunks."

Does your choice of artistic impression have the rings to match your life experiences? The rings on trees tell what the tree has gone through, how long it's lived, and what weather it's lived through. Does your art convey your loneliness, pain, or love? Does it show the storms you've weathered or the life you've lived?

Or, does your work express nothing.

Will it be like chopping down a tree only to find the inside is hollow and worthless? If you paint a portrait, does it contain an aspect of yourself in the art? Or are you just making a reproduction of someone else's observations? Are you even worth the paper you print on?

Photographers have refined monotony into its purest strain of boredom. Not only have they abandoned originality, but they've also memorialized its antithesis. Sit exactly like this, right here, in this seasonal prop stage that I built to pump out twenty identical sessions, just like one, all in one day only to repeat it all tomorrow as well. I even know what to say and what prompts to give to get the appropriate emotional response to make this an even more sterile set of smiling images. By the way, the only emotion allowed to express in popular photography is happiness and love. All other emotions get tossed by the wayside.

Chapter Three

"The picture is not made by the photographer, the picture is more good or less good in function of the relationship that you have with the people you photograph."
-Sebastiao Salgado

Admit it, you are absolute garbage at relationships. You're a poor communicator. You're unrelatable, unstable, and hard to digest. Maybe you're just uninterested so you don't even bother to put forth the effort.

No, I'm not recounting the latest gossip I heard from your ex. I'm talking about your relationship to your art, to the clients you work with, to the tools you use to create. If you're a photographer, do you have the best and newest gear? Why? Do you throw away your favorite paintbrush every time you get a new set, or does that old one just feel right in your hands?

You're not going to build a relationship with your subject doing twenty " $50 Christmas mini-sessions" each day. You're just treating them the same as the props you're going to toss into your vehicle at the end of the day. The only difference is you spend more time with your props. You're also not going to build a relationship by looking at a flower once and deciding to paint one. You don't get to know your tools by worrying about the newest or what everyone else is using either. Tools should be familiar to you, second nature, just like engaging in social relationships with other human beings.

Relationships are about time invested, and depth of interest. If you're not interested in your relationship then you're not going to invest the time. If you don't invest the time your art is going to be bland and not even an accurate display of your subject.

This goes even further when you bring in the lack of empathy that comes with non-relational art. Just today I saw a photographer using a portrait of a recently deceased client to climb up on a pedestal and harp about how important it is to schedule family portraits. My guy, a person is literally dead and your first thought is *rubs hands together* "This is going to make such a great piece of ad copy."

Unfortunately seeing this barely made me do a double-take. I've seen so much exploitation used as common marketing that it's been normalized and accepted in the community.

Without relational art, we go about treating all of our art as work, and when it's all work it becomes detached from emotion and we become this corporate amalgamation that's just as toxic as the oil companies that can't seem to keep their product in the container. The only difference is instead of oil-slicked wildfowl, you're slowly killing the people and relationships around you and all in the pursuit of profits.

If you chase profits, you're going to hurt people. If you chase relationships, the profits come naturally.

"We live in a society where we never prepare people to be a community." -Sebastiao Salgado

Art is about being a better individual so that you can be better at relationships, and be a better part of the community. Art shouldn't leave you or your subject the same. When you finish a painting you've finished revealing something about yourself, and when you finish up a photography shoot, you should be better for the interaction.

"Blah blah blah, Michael we get it. You hate successful artists and are an absolute purist when it comes to making money."

I mean, yes and no. I understand that money makes the world go round. I know that it's nicer to eat a well-balanced and well-earned meal than it is to nibble on acrylic paints and lacquered canvas or memory cards and aperture blades. I also understand that for an artist to be self-sustaining they either need to create work that conforms to a marketable aesthetic, or they need to sideline their art and place it secondary to the job that actually will sustain their living needs.

However, what I'm talking about, and what I think I hate most, is that there are entire groups specifically designed for belittling other artists. On social media, there are entire groups designed to make fun of anything from your wedding ring, wedding dress, tattoos, architecture, portraits, clients, paintings, etc. If it's been created by someone, there's a group to make fun of it, or the creator, simply for not conforming to what the majority find aesthetically pleasing. This isn't just confined to the internet though. Hardly. I'd go so far as to say the internet is just a symptom of the same people that gather and make these crushing judgments in real life. After all, what is the internet besides just a gathering of all those people?

The only benefit to these kinds of internet groups is that they're usually honest and transparent about their intent. Meanwhile, the other cliques will disguise themselves as groups of support and learning, yet the result is always the same. "40-year" veteran creatives working to homogenize the influx of new creators and new creatives working to weasel their way into the successful group of elites by putting down their peers and "otherize" them. "Sure, I'm new, but I'm not THAT new."

Well, to the veteran creatives: You can't homogenize me, I'm not your cow, and my art isn't your milk so kindly get off my tits.

And for the "New but not that new crowd", grow up and stop acting like this is some middle school clique. You know you can form your own identity outside of using the bones of others to frame it up right?

This is what happens when we become fully detached from empathy and our relational art. We become nasty, bitter, selfish, backstabbing, and petty humans that cut off any outside connection that doesn't immediately mesh with our sense of what's correct, standard, aesthetic, or proper.

Jumping over with a palate cleanser: Did you know that in 1989 Andres Serrano's "Piss Christ" (Literally a photograph of a crucifix in a jar of his urine.) started a congressional debate on US public arts funding and US Senators publicly denounced his work? Yes, I just cleansed your mental palate with some urine art.

Robert Mapplethorpe had his exhibition canceled a month before its debut in 1989 because it depicted explicit acts of homosexuality and other taboo subjects including images of anal fisting. Again, congressmen who had control of the funding of the National Endowment for the Arts played a role in this censorship. (The Washington Project for the Arts came together with some private contributors and brought the exhibition to DC anyway.)

More recently I heard of a Mayor in Florida threatening to cut funding to an art exhibit unless two of the artists were dropped from the roster because he believed them to be "sympathetic towards communism."

On that same note, creative artist Sally Mann has been actively protested and worked against for the majority of her career. From religious groups and conservatives claiming that her photographs of her children, in her work titled "Immediate Family", were equal to child pornography, to galleries canceling the showings of her body of work titled "What Remains" for being too disturbing.

It could be easily suggested that Sally Mann's bodies of work could have been snuffed out early on had she indulged the vocal majority in producing more aesthetically acceptable imagery. I'm sure that if I were to produce a body of work today consisting entirely of images of decomposing corpses it would at best be shunned by the local community, and at worst censored and my intentions and mental health publicly questioned.

Just last year, Christopher Mckenney, a surrealist photographer and artist posted an image in February 2020 of a crimson-robed figure resembling a Klan member with slogans adorning the robes such as "Make America Great Again". A powerful statement, and an obvious jab at then-president Donald Trump. Minutes after posting I saw the comments flooded with infuriated Trump supporters and people claiming to be fans of art but not "this" kind of art.

Often people who don't understand the roots of art will be quick to disavow any art that challenges their worldview but perfectly fine consuming art that aligns with their own. Despite that being the entire objective of art. To challenge worldviews, prompt discussion, evoke emotion and bring about change.
At this time I believe the image was pulled from Facebook but can still be found on his Twitter

I'd certainly be in the wrong if I failed to mention the numerous George Floyd murals and art pieces done in remembrance and protest, along with the Black Lives Matter movement, and the effect it had on the art world as well. The arts and politics have been intertwined since the inception of both. Both as a method of social change, and as a countercultural force of power. These voices stem from a place of relational empathy within the arts.

However, as to the effects of non-relational art and to draw a more direct correlation between all of these artists and what I'm talking about with the homogenization of new artists: There is blatant censorship happening but we would never call it censorship. We call it standards. We label it as "quality".

I suppose we differentiate between our power as a collective voice stifling creativity, and the systematic power of a governing body weighing its force to censor but they hold the same weight and the same destructive force.

Again, somewhere along the lines we lost our artistic voice and traded our groundbreaking images for fairytale moments only.

I'm looking at you, wedding photographers, and your related ilk. Am I saying that wedding photography isn't art? I'm not sure I'd like to say that, there are certainly some wedding photographers that create art within the niche, but I will say that, without a doubt, it's not to the same level as Charles Moore's 1963 Birmingham Alabama civil rights protest images.

Or for that matter Chris Hondros's 2005 images of Samar Hassan at a military checkpoint after losing both of her parents to American soldiers who believed Iraqi rebels were in their car.

Diane Arbus said: "I really believe there are things nobody would see if I didn't photograph them."
Art is supposed to expose the dark nooks and crannies where the normal individual doesn't go or know what to look for.

Though wedding photographers and family portrait artists often seem to take their positions so seriously, as if the entire art industry revolves around what they do, I often find it to be about the most menial and disinteresting in the creative and artistic realm. It's becoming assembly line work for the stagnant creative mind.

Or in the words of Sebastiao Salgado:

"Photography has become a small world with so many jealous people. You do a story and then a lot of people try to do the same thing."

I mean, don't get me wrong. The clients I've had over the years have been some of the most amazing friends I could ever have asked for, and indeed their weddings were beautiful, and some of the work that makes me most proud comes from those same weddings. However, my work wasn't curing cancer. It wasn't the end all be all of the artistic realms, and fighting to stay creative in that closed niche is one of the things that both challenged me, and got me hired for those jobs.

Give me the LSD-fueled ramblings, neon paint splatters on cardboard and emotionally charged art pieces any day over the highly processed and sterilized images of a lone depiction of a hand on canvas or yet another smiling child portrait to hang forgotten in a dusty foyer somewhere.

I know my writing is heavily photography-centric, but I warned you early on where the bulk of my experience stands so pardon me, or don't, I don't care. If you can't draw the inference and apply it to your craft then maybe reread it until it sticks or something, I don't know.

Music as an art form has been no exception to this either. The glossy radio hits we hear today are simultaneously paired with the censored music of yesterday. The Pink Floyd's, Led Zeppelin's, Nirvana, and the Rage Against The Machine of yesteryear. Though now deemed culturally acceptable, upon release they were shunned, threatened with lawsuits, and received heavy political and social pushback.

More than ever I see unintentional or aimless art as a squandered opportunity. We are so, incredibly, ridiculously, and enormously privileged beyond anything that makes sense. To be able to have the mindset for

creativity is a rewarding gift. To make visual art that speaks to the cultural, emotional, and political soul of society. To produce work that doesn't encapsulate any of these things is a waste of not only your time but of all our time.
"As if you could kill time without injuring eternity." -Henry David Thoreau

Chapter Four

"I don't want anyone to appreciate the light or the palette of tones. I want my pictures to inform, to provoke discussion – and to raise money"

If your art isn't revolutionary I don't want any part of it. Or in the words of Emma Goldman - "If I can't dance, I don't want to be part of your revolution."

A revolution is progress or a movement that changes the standard system of things. The current standing of the arts is slowly rotting from the insides like that time you snuck out late with friends and drank that "tasty" bottle of Mad Dog 20/20, and that can of four loco, but forgot that you had to exist the next day.

Now, why am I all of a sudden talking about revolution? Am I encouraging you to go print seditious materials and overthrow your local government? Yes. I mean, no, no, of course not. No, the revolution I'm talking about is about changing your local art community of course. Change starts from the ground up. So, if all the things I'm complaining about are to change at all, it's going to start at home. It's going to start with you and I can't do it by myself.

Here's an idea: Get off of the internet. That's it. Sign off. You can do this. When's the last time you even showered? No, I mean like REALLY showered? Did you know that there are people right in your neighborhood for you to connect to? Like, you probably even have a neighbor. I can't tell for sure, but I'm just going out on a limb here. Open the curtains, throw on sunglasses if you need to. Whatever you do, just get out there into the thick of it.

See, art is about connection, and your art isn't going to work all that well if you isolate inside your little agoraphobic bubble, you absolute filth ball. Again, speaking from experience here. Did I mention I'm agoraphobic?

We're so wound up in the SEO, the Facebook ads, the Google ads, and my God if I have to hear one more person ask why they aren't getting an Instagram interaction I may walk out into traffic. Youtube? Squarespace sponsorship? Content creators certainly create content, but what real value does it contain?

When is the last time you took your art to the local gathering spot and shook hands with the people purchasing it? When's the last time you took a fledgling artist under your wing and gave them the materials and confidence to produce work. I'm not talking about teaching them how to regurgitate your work, but giving them the resources and ability to make their own, whatever it may be, despite whether you enjoy it or not. Creating can be cathartic, and their work doesn't need to benefit you at all.

Despite everything you're going to be told about marketing online, the truth is that your online marketing sucks because you suck at people. Meeting people broadens your mind, and broadening your mind, aside from not making you such a dull half-wit, broadens the scope and depth that you can create from.

I'm laying in kind of hard here. Lemme take a step back and we'll trudge through my first artistic endeavors some fourteen to fifteen years ago.

I started with a film photography course in high school where we learned to shoot and develop black and white film, along with making our own pinhole cameras. I was excruciatingly bad. The majority of my shots were either so under or overexposed that no image could be pulled. The other images were just out-of-focus images of trees or corners of buildings in an attempt to be abstract and "artsy". The thing is, I loved that class, and my teacher never had a negative word to say about any of the absolute garbage I put on their desk.

Despite doing well and thoroughly enjoying the class, when I graduated I didn't keep up with it because I didn't know you could buy chemicals and develop your film. The next year however I picked up a cheap Sony Cybershot from somewhere and I was back at it taking pictures of mushrooms, trees, you name it. Still really bad, but on reflection, I had decided that I should try to make money so I could keep doing this. I wanted to make enough to sustain my passion. However, and with good intentions, a friend was quick to let me know that the camera was just never going to be good enough to do any kind of "professional" work.

Feeling defeated I put the camera down for a while until I bought my first "professional" camera.
In early 2012 I was working part-time for just above minimum wage, renting a house with bills that exceeded my income, and dealing with the idea that I was rowing a boat uphill. With no substantial income for extra purchases or savings, I came up with a largely frivolous idea. I wanted to buy that "professional" camera.

Up until this point I had carried around my point and shoots, and cell phone cameras, but I was ready to be serious about learning this art. I put a broken Marshall amp that my father had bought for me, on eBay for $800. Nothing, not a single bite. Then for $700, again, nothing. I put the amp back up in a last-ditch effort again for $600 and about an hour later I received a message from a person interested in purchasing and restoring the amp. $500, top offer.

I sold, packaged, and shipped the amp that day. Logged into my eBay account and found the first "real" camera I could find, an old Canon XT camera with the kit 18-55mm lens, bag, and accessories. And my photography journey started…. And I have to reiterate again and again how much I really, really sucked. Like, I was surprisingly bad. On the plus side though I photographed everything and brought the camera everywhere with me. It became my best friend, and my coping mechanism through periods of unemployment, divorce, homelessness. I bought old lenses for cheap, rummaged about at pawn shops and yard sales looking for dusty deals. I began doing small shoots for friends including maternity, newborn, landscape, engagements, and even second shooting a few weddings.

It became a natural appendage for me, like another set of eyes to view the world in a calmer and more focused way. Through my introversion the camera allowed me to interact with others, to experience their moments of joy, happiness, and love. It gave me the chance to document things that I would have otherwise disqualified myself from experiencing.

When my high school dog passed away I was able to look at the pictures I had of her. When my grandfather passed away I was able to dig through the digital library and pull images I had taken from visits with him. When my father passed away however it was a real struggle to find images that I had of him. He had managed to provide the ability for my picture obsession but he was rather reclusive as is and was never quite fond of me shoving a camera in his face for pictures. So I was left with only a couple.

Fortunately for the traditions of the past, I was given a Tupperware container of images of my father as a teenager and from the years during and after my birth. Precious photos that preserve the memory of my dad in a physical form. Looking back, the small action of my dad buying me a guitar amp as a teenager resulted in my ability to buy a camera, and eventually that camera led me to a point of self-sufficiency. It changed the way I view life. When I'm photographing weddings, family portraits, and newborn photos, I know these are the memories that will be preserved long after the people in the photos are gone.

I'm under no disillusion that my father knew that a purchase like that would ripple and affect the way I live years down the road, but that doesn't stop me from being thankful. And somewhere out there, someone is rocking out on a loud amp. I don't consider those images art either, by the way. Beautiful, cherished memories of my father, but snapshots and by no means taken to be some greater work or emotional experience.

Anyway, enough sentimental mess and back to that super professional Canon XT. At half the megapixels and twice the size, I continued taking trash images. Nobody told me that my lack of focus, of creative vision, was the issue, just that I needed better gear. So, I started joining groups, they'd critique my images, tell me where to refine my images, and also gawk at my bad camera. So, again, I upgraded my camera, and this time I bought new lenses as well.

The thing is, I was still really bad and none of this was stuff that I wanted to photograph, it's just what would pay me. I had completely shelved my idea of making abstract images and art, and despite that being what brought me joy, I had transitioned into chasing the dream of being a full-time "artist". Instead of art, of course, I mean I was a person with a camera. I don't think most people get past this point. They may get better with their camera, or get a better camera, just like someone gets better at painting, or gets better brushes, but they aren't a painter or an artist.

They're just people with tools of the trade. They never choose their focus and fit money into that, they instead try to cram their focus into where the money is at, and doing this they give up any real creative feeling and release. You can be a great photographer and a terrible artist. You can be a great painter and a terrible artist. The problem is, you can't be a great artist and be terrible with your tools.

You can change your methods and tools to make up for where you fall short though, but this doesn't work in reverse. Better tools won't make you a better photographer. They can help you overcome artistic handicaps, sure.

Anyway, fast forward another decade, because that's how long it took me to try and transition away from being a good photographer and back into being a fledgling artist. I wish somewhere earlier along that journey someone would have pulled me aside and told me to go back to what I loved. Get a couple of side jobs and make art just for making art.

When I finally made the decision to do the kind of photography I wanted to do, and mold it into the kind of photography I was already doing, that's when I finally found a profitable groove anyway. My photography became less focused on close-up wedding portraits and became more about the environment and story in the rest of the image. Clients loved it and sought us out for that difference in style.

Finding my artistic voice made me a better photographer almost overnight.

Chapter Five

"No, it's not a very good story - its author was too busy listening to other voices to listen as closely as he should have to the one coming from inside."- Stephen King

Lemme just take this time to go on a tirade about breaking out of the cult of normalcy you were brainwashed into that would make even a college philosophy professor blush.

Throw off with reckless abandon the shackles of artistic rules ingrained into the listed dos and don'ts that you've formed in your mind. You need to go and get lost in a tangent. With everything you learn in art, there comes a point where being so critical just becomes the millstone dragging your apathetic body down to the depths of mediocrity, into unstimulated burnout, and if left unattended, into a slow and unannounced regression of abilities.

Like a bike that's been left unridden for long enough, the chain begins to rust, the tires go flat and dry rot, and then the day comes for it to perform again, discovered upon like a long lost friend from elementary school, only to realize the bike is in shambles, and the relationship made shallow by neglect.

That's right, now you're a rusty bike! Analogies are pretty cool like that. Earlier you were a lot of other names I called you, but now you've been reduced to an inanimate object that's not even in good shape. Story of your life I'm sure. Oh well, I don't make the rules.

You'll find you've perfected your craft right into shambles. With anxious hands and in an attempt to be "different", "new", or "edgy", you'll fall back on the old habits of the past, repeating your beginner habits in an attempt to make "art" again.

You won't realize that these things can be done differently, that they can be made into something quite beautiful, no, you won't realize this because, at the peak of Dunning-Kruger, you've planted your flag like some kind of oblivious astronaut touching down in Alabama and thinking you made it to outer space.

You have ascended to the highest hill of "are we there yet" only to think you've made it to that final place with no room left to expand. The educational ropes you used to climb the challenges of early-stage art have become the bindings that hold your wrists back from breaking molds and adventuring into the unknown.

And the greatest disservice was that through all of your learning, improvements, and profits, you locked yourself in a box, and built walls to keep the box out.

Getting lost in a tangent, for me, happens quite often, and often to my partner's dismay. Pretty sure I just had one right there a few sentences up. Anyway, I'll storm in with thoughts going a thousand miles an hour and start pouring words out like a busted pipe. (Being bipolar and having frequent manic episodes doesn't help either. Oh, and ADHD, I'm almost positive I haven't mentioned ADHD yet. I'll blame that on ADHD.)

Being lost in a tangent is about being so in love with the story, the idea, and the craft, that it excited you to the point of restlessness, thinking and rethinking details and future ideas and all the many possibilities. Writing this book has been done in multiple six to eight-hour full-on writing sessions because once the idea hit I just couldn't get good sleep until I'd worked on it.

It's also being so lost in the craft that things like uncooperative clients don't phase you, you're too in your thoughts, in your viewfinder, canvas, craft, moving to get the next shot, the next brushstroke, the next hundred words, and all the while cramming down the last slice of day-old pizza because you need the calories but can't be bothered caring about anything else.

Now for some math time! My favorite. Not really, I'm pretty sure I either failed or almost failed math every year in Highschool. Fortunately for all of us, this is basic addition and some easy division.

There are sixty minutes in an hour, sixty seconds in a minute which means if you're a photographer, that's shooting at 1/250'th of a second, in each hour you have nine-hundred thousand frames of possibility you can capture. Each hour of your day is filled with split-second stories that you can either document or let melt back into time. We often don't think of these, or at least, we don't think to apply these ideas, even as photographers whose job it is to document stories and moments.

A friend mentioned that they were asked out to breakfast by a client but it was unfortunate as mornings weren't exactly their thing (see where I said being relational and getting a shower and leaving your cave was a necessary part of art?), which is when I originally put forward the above "frames per hour idea". I even went as far as to figure out the average distance from one side of a diner booth, to the other, so I could work out the room they would have with a fifty-millimeter lens.

The friend reminded me this was just breakfast with a client, not a shoot. It's times like this where the things that come into my mind surprise even me, not because they should be surprising, but for the exact opposite reason, it makes so much sense.

"Are you a photographer, or do you just take pictures for work?"

We tend to find ourselves having made art for so long that the initial excitement blends into the background under all of the learning, the skills, the guidelines, and the outlines of how or when we "should" do things like photography. The thing about all of this is, we didn't get into our creative niche because we love planning meetings, keeping records, and managing bookings, and doing our accounting.

Typically we get into art because we love CREATING something. We want to capture moments, or emotions, or a raw idea, something we can't quite place our finger on. Sometimes we just need to create because it's what calms us. It's our mental catharsis. We need that reminder that we are photographers, we are creators, we are artists we don't just DO art.

Here's another thing, even if you wanted to be some assembly line creative, you couldn't be if you tried. People are biased. YOU'RE biased. No pineapple doesn't belong on pizza and if you think differently then you can meet me in Denny's parking lot and square the hell up.

This is something that some philosophers and psychologists would insist is inevitable. (The bias, not us fighting in Denny's parking lot. That's only inevitable if you bring me pineapple on a pizza.) Bias is inevitably inherent in your psyche whether you want to acknowledge it or not.

I don't know, I'm not a psychologist, however much that career path would have made my parents happier and me a bit wealthier. It is because of this inherent bias that you cannot "capture" a moment. Not with your camera, not with your pen, not with your brush on a canvas.

It's more often than not that you are documenting moments as you perceive them, through the biased lens of your eyes. This is why the entire point of art isn't to make a reproduction. Even your memories aren't accurate no matter how much you swear you only had three beers last night.

As a matter of fact, you should probably cut back some on the alcohol. Between this and the earlier mad dog 20/20/four loco incident, I'm starting to think you may have a bit of a problem.

Art is about stories, stories of the people involved, stories about yourself and the way you interact with the world, and the way the world interacts with you.

The benefit of these stories is that they will make you a better person. Once you've figured out, heard, and seen someone's story, come to understand your own story, you'll feel empathy for that person and those people. Seeing the stories of people crushes ideas of prejudice, these ideas you've unconsciously and consciously formed about strangers, and by doing this, they aren't strangers.

If you spend your entire artistic career trying to be good at being normal, you'll never realize your own story, which means you'll continue to be really sucky at relationships, and really sucky at empathizing with the stories of others that you're trying to tell.

Chapter Six

"Expression is never helped by suppression."-Deng Ming-Dao

Let's be honest for a minute. You're creatively constipated. Ugh. Backed up by weeks, to months, to possibly years of unused creative juices just waiting for a chance to be put to use.

Please god, let me never have to write something like "juices" and "constipated" again. I'm no doctor but this just seems like a terrible combination.

Example time. I was just watching an interview with Billie Eilish (don't judge me, her music slaps) and she made a statement that all the famous artists that we see are sad. She was referring to her fellow musicians of course, but it seemed like a serious statement with some merit behind it so I went to look for myself to see if there is a consensus on this, and there kinda is.

I know out of the artists I know personally (you'll have to live with my anecdotal evidence) a good majority of them go through reclusive bouts and manic stages of creativity and the running joke is "we're all a bit messed up". From what I've been able to find though, we might actually BE a bit messed up. (I mean, again, I'm Bipolar, ADHD, did I mention agoraphobic? How about GAD? Probably not but now you know one more of my dazzling titles. If I did… just blame it on my ADHD.)

"In the case of unipolar or major depression, the population rate is about 5% but the rate among artists and writers in the various studies is between 15% and 50%."

One of the ideas behind the "why" of this seems to be that to be creatively minded we

1. Have these bouts of reclusiveness and self-reflection which could make us more prone to being overly analytical of ourselves as well as

2. "our openness to new experiences, tolerance for ambiguity, and the way we approach life enables us to perceive things in a fresh and novel way. Less creative types "quickly respond to situations based on what they have been told by people in authority", while creatives live in a more fluid and nebulous (read: incredibly stressful) world.

"Such traits can lead to feelings of depression or social alienation,"

By the way, I'd like, totally cite the sources for all these quotes here, but the entire webpage is gone now which kinda made writing this section a pain in my ass. Now it can be a pain in yours to verify I'm not just lying to you. Good luck!

I'd wonder if intertwining the creative mentality with also being a professional 24/7 and also never getting the time to create paired with the advent of social media would compound the pressure.

I've seen photographers and other artists mention that once they started their businesses they felt like they couldn't speak or act as openly anymore. Primarily the fear seems to be that the repercussions would be either losing clients who didn't agree with their viewpoints regardless of it being art or that they'd be viewed as less than reputable for taking a stance on absolutely anything.

This seems really at odds with how the arts have been utilized historically. Throughout history, the arts have had a multi-faceted use. This kind of art can be traced back as far as what we would now consider ancient times. Sculptures and paintings were used as symbols of power by the wealthy and used as a voice for the oppressed to speak through. Instead, artists are now becoming voluntarily spineless in the name of profits. The integrity of their art comes second.

Art has the ability to sway public and political opinion. Possibly no greater example of this could be seen than the World War Two propaganda that was displayed on both sides of the conflict. Any wartime propaganda could be referenced here but I think World War Two is the most well known.

Yet with all that said most modern artists either don't consider their opinions valuable enough to voice or feel like having an opinion, taking a stance, will hurt them more than helping them in the long run.

Unfortunately, my personal opinion is that it's the exact opposite. You're repressing your creativity is what's hurting you the most. Possibly quite literally. So like…it's time to take some creative Miralax and… relieve yourself of the creative burden.

Some extended cut, director's edition, style thoughts here.

Earlier I talked about how I hated the backbiting and negativity of the art community. So, you may have asked, or be asking me now, what's my solution? What's my utopian vision of the art community look like? That's pretty easy for me to sum up. "The Inklings."

If you're unfamiliar with the inklings, they were a group of primarily fiction authors that met together between the 1930s and 1950. The most well-known of them are probably C.S Lewis and J.R.R Tolkein. Though, their ranks held a plethora of authors, professors, and exceptionally brilliant creatives and intellectuals.

What made the inklings special, to me anyway, was that it was a community that they had built around their art, and dedicated to their art, and the advancement and refinement of it. Heated discussions took place I'm sure, but their goal was pretty simple. They'd get together at the same pub, kick back some brews, and they'd put their art on display for one another to appreciate and add pointers to.

The objective wasn't to belittle or break each other's spirit, and it also wasn't to refine the works so that they all shared the same feeling and style.
Each of them specialized in their areas and the growth wasn't towards anything but progress.

With that said, start small. Build a community around your art. I'm not just talking about clients that appreciate and purchase your art. I'm talking about gathering a small network of fellow artists and craft makers that all share the same ideal of cooperative growth and success. They don't have to like your work, agree with your work, or financially support your work. Their goal is to support you as a creative. To prod you along to be the most self-actualized and best representation of yourself.

The community should have a secondary goal outside of self-actualization. Your community should enrich the greater community. Referring back to an early quote by Salgado: "I don't want anyone to appreciate the light or the palette of tones. I want my pictures to inform, to provoke discussion - and to raise money."

Relationships are about enrichment. Enriching yourself, your soul, but also enriching those around you. With your art and art community, you can fund local charities. You can help fund and build local infrastructure. Hell, Salgado built an entire rainforest providing habitat to thousands of animals, many on the endangered list. Where once a desert was, now a thriving natural resource has been replenished and is thriving.

He quite literally enriched his community and you can do the same thing through your art and your relationship with your surroundings.

In closing this thing out, why are you still here? Don't you have something to start creating? Did you not take anything I just said to heart? Don't you have hands to shake, bridges to build, forests to plant, the hungry to feed?

Go create something. Make it ugly. Make it weird. Make it poorly, make it beautiful and unique. You're only failing if you're not trying. Stagnation is the worst kind of death.

In a Sally Mann interview that I watched recently, she quotes her friend Jim Lewis saying "An asshole who makes great art, is an asshole that makes great art but an asshole who makes bad art is just an asshole." I'm used to being the latter, I've spent years being called one. So, my only real goal with my work, and with this book as a standalone piece of art, is to be the former.

You're STILL here? To the very end? You know this isn't a Youtube giveaway video right? You're not going to find some hidden code down here to enter into your escape room. Your door is only locked from the inside. At least, I hope so.

Well, I'll give you something for sticking around this long anyway. How about a checklist of things you can do to contribute art within your local community?

Some Ideas:

- ☐ Create or join a community shared art space
  Community art spaces are a great place to meet fellow artists, support peers, and establish a safe space for growth and relationships.

- ☐ Create or join an art mentoring program
  The arts aren't accessible to everyone but they could be if you got off your ass and made them accessible.

- ☐ Display and sell your work at Second Sunday/community yard sale gatherings.
  This is more about the networking and community support so go light on the selling and heavy on the displaying and handshaking.

- ☐ Hang your work at places for free such as local coffee shops
  The keyword here is free. Free art beautifies local businesses, draws in customers for the atmosphere, and can raise awareness of your work.

- [ ] Ask to paint local murals around the community or hang metal prints of your photography or sculpt art for the community.

- [ ] Establish or join in on community art projects
  You may need to get to work with your local city hall and government organizations but if you pitch the right deal you could be painting and arting up the town!

- [ ] Join or found a community art club
  You can make club shirts, raise money for the community and for the community art projects to beautify your neighborhood!

- [ ] Always photograph art events.
  Even if you're not the photographer, if you can't find one to volunteer, take the images yourself. Publicity helps spread awareness.

- [ ] Immerse yourself in local art.
  Maybe you aren't the social butterfly. If you haven't gathered it already, neither am I. However, no worries, there's still room for you in the community. Sometimes the best thing you can do is just be there. Just appreciate the art and let the artists know you've got their backs.

- [ ] Community gardens and planting trees
  Get dirty while expanding nature. If you don't think gardening is an art form then I dare say you've never made fresh Bruschetta from the ingredients you grew yourself. Get to work making food! Excess food can also be donated to local food banks and shelters as long as they have a long enough lifespan left. If not, get to preserving and pickling and donate those!

- [ ] If All else fails, go to Pinterest and find collaborative art projects you can do within your community.

IT'S STILL BUILLSH*T

www.ingramcontent.com/pod-product-compliance
Lightning Source LLC
Chambersburg PA
CBHW070139230526
45472CB00004B/1601